MW01632404

The Tennessee Bucket List

100 Ways to Have a
Real Tennessee
Experience

Michael Crisp

REMIX BOOKS

Published in Georgetown, KY

United States of America

Remix Books
PO Box 1303
Georgetown, KY 40324

www.facebook.com/TheTennesseeBucketList

Cover Design and Layout by
Kevin Kifer
www.k2-technology.com

ISBN 978-1-6284-7546-3

First Edition

legal disclaimer

This book is designed to provide information, entertainment, and motivation to our readers. It is sold with the understanding that the publisher is not engaged to render any type of physical, psychological, legal, or any other advice.

Participation in the activities listed may be dangerous, illegal, and could lead to arrest, serious injury, or death.

The content in this book is the sole expression and opinion of its author and not necessarily that of the publisher. No warranties or guarantees are expressed or implied.

Neither the publisher nor the author shall be liable for any physical, psychological, emotional, financial, or commercial damages, including, but not limited to, special, incidental, consequential, or other damages.

Our views and rights are the same: you are responsible for your own choices, actions, and results.

President Andrew Jackson.
Photo courtesy the Library of Congress

dedication

For Ketch, Critter, Gill, Morgan, Kevin, Cory and Chance. Your music makes the bad times better and the good times great.

bucket list:

a number of experiences or achievements that a person hopes to have or accomplish during their lifetime.

Courtesy of the Oxford American Dictionary

Breathtaking. That's the first word that comes to mind when I think of Tennessee. While driving, or better yet, walking through the state, you can't help but be amazed by all of its natural beauty.

Tennessee is a state that is filled with incredible sights, sounds, and experiences, and selecting only a hundred of them for this book was a challenge indeed. But within this book, I have selected the ultimate list of adventures that are essential to anyone who is in search of a true Tennessee experience.

While writing this book, I came across a handful of items that helped me with my research. There were several websites devoted to traveling in Tennessee, most notably tnvacation.com, which offered a handful of wonderful suggestions that I added to the list.

One of the biggest inspirations for this book is my good friend, David Sloan. David is an author (and all-around renaissance man) who resides in Key West, Florida. David wrote The Key West Bucket List, which met with great success. Last year he convinced me (rather easily) to write The Kentucky Bucket List, a book that allowed me to combine two of my passions, writing and travel.

Whether you are from Tennessee, live here now, or are planning a visit, I hope that you enjoy this book and the experiences that are within it.

what to expect

1. No Instruction Manual:

This book isn't an instructional guidebook that tells you what to do and how to do it. The object here is for you to seek out each of the items in this book and then enjoy these experiences on your own.

2. Adventure and Challenge:

Some of the items on this list are easy to accomplish, some are more difficult, and others are downright close to impossible. Don't worry - no one is watching you or grading your performance. Take each adventure one by one, at your own pace, and you will get the most out of this book.

3. Inspiration:

I've often been accused of being a "know-it-all" (especially after I've had a few cold beverages), but I'm definitely not a fountain of wisdom. That's why I called in the experts. Mark Twain, Helen Keller, William Shakespeare and Abraham Lincoln are all contributors with quotes that lend a deeper meaning to each adventure.

4. Satisfaction:

Whether you take the time to fill out the list at the end of this book, or you take each of these journeys in your mind from the comfort of your favorite chair, this book should leave you with a profound sense of satisfaction. You will have so much fun with this book that you'll probably feel like sharing your own thoughts and stories with others. Feel free to visit our Facebook page to share your musings, experiences, photos, and new additions to the list.

Enjoy,
Michael Crisp

"The true adventurer goes forth aimless and uncalculating to meet and greet unknown fate."

- O. Henry

1

See a Show at the Grand Ole Opry

Grand Ole Opry House, Nashville

"Carnegie Hall was real fabulous, but you know, it ain't as big as the Grand Ole Opry."

- Patsy Cline

2

Behold the Beauty of a Tennessee Walker

Tennessee Walking Horse National Celebration, Shelbyville

"I've often said there's nothing better for the inside of a man than the outside of a horse."

- Ronald Reagan

3

Camp Out Under the Stars

Fort Pillow State Park, Henning

"Aim for the moon. If you miss, you may hit a star."

- W. Clement Stone

4

Soak in the Hot Tub of a Rented Chalet

Anywhere in the Smoky Mountains

"Women are like teabags. We don't know our true strength until we are in hot water."

- Eleanor Roosevelt

5

Watch a NASCAR™ Race

Bristol Motor Speedway, Bristol

"Fix your eyes on perfection and you make almost everything speed towards it."

- William Ellery Channing

6

Sip Moonshine

Anywhere, but Preferably With Good Friends

"We are here and it is now. Further than that, all human knowledge is moonshine."

- H.L. Mencken

7

Wander The District

The District, Nashville

"There's a magical tie to the land of our home, which the heart cannot break, though the footsteps may roam."

- Eliza Cook

8

Explore a King's Mansion

Graceland, Memphis

"From the time I was a kid, I always knew something was going to happen to me. Didn't know exactly what."

- Elvis Presley

9

Be a Part of an Archeological Dig

Gray Fossil Site, Jonesborough

"Let others praise ancient times; I am glad I was born in these."

- Ovid

10

See a Civil War Reenactment

Stones River National Battlefield,
Murfreesboro

"A battle lost or won is easily described, understood, and appreciated, but the moral growth of a great nation requires reflection, as well as observation, to appreciate it."

- Frederick Douglass

11

Enjoy a Goo Goo Cluster™

Goo Goo Outpost at Fontanel, Nashville

"All you need is love. But a little chocolate now and then doesn't hurt."

- Charles M. Schulz

12

See Seven States at the Same Time

Rock City, Lookout Mountain

"It's easier to go down a hill than up it, but the view is much better at the top."

- Henry Ward Beecher

13

Go Fly Fishing in Flat Fork Creek

Frozen Head State Park, Wartburg

"If fishing is a religion, fly fishing is high church."

- Tom Brokaw

14

Search for the Bell Witch

Adams

"Double, double, toil and trouble, fire burn and cauldron bubble."

- William Shakespeare

15

Take Your Family to the Pink Palace

The Pink Palace Family of Museums, Memphis

"If you cannot get rid of the family skeleton, you may as well make it dance."

- George Bernard Shaw

The Pink Palace, Memphis
Photo courtesy of The Pink Palace

16

Take a Walk Down Music Row

16th Avenue and 17th Avenue, Nashville

"A woman's two cents worth is worth two cents in the music business."

- Loretta Lynn

17

Visit the Home of Davy Crockett

Davy Crockett Birthplace State Park, Greeneville

"Let your tongue speak what your heart thinks."

- Davy Crockett

18

See a Panda Bear

Memphis Zoo, Memphis

"I love acting, but it's much more fun taking kids to the zoo."

- Nicole Kidman

19

Devour a Bible Burger

Tinsley-Bible Drugstore, Dandridge

"I like mine with lettuce and tomato, Heinz 57 and french-fried potatoes."

- Jimmy Buffett

20

Drive Under a Covered Bridge

Doe River Covered Bridge, Elizabethton

"A politician is a man who will double cross that bridge when he comes to it."

- Oscar Levant

Union Cemetery, Shiloh National Military Park
Photo courtesy of the Library of Congress

21

Walk the Field at Shiloh

Shiloh National Military Park, Shiloh

"War is hell."

- General William T. Sherman

22

Explore Cades Cove

Great Smoky Mountains National Park,
Townsend

"In wisdom gathered over time I have found that every experience is a form of exploration."

- Ansel Adams

23

Stroll Down Beale Street

Memphis

"A woman drove me to drink and I didn't even have the decency to thank her."

- W.C. Fields

24

See the Sunsphere

World's Fair Park, Knoxville

"The time to repair the roof is when the sun is shining."

- John F. Kennedy

The Sunsphere at the World's Fair Park, Knoxville
Photo courtesy of Jeffrey Paul Prickett of ineighborhood.info

25

Buy a Pair of Boots

Katy K's Ranch Dressing, Nashville

"A lie can be halfway round the world before the truth has got its boots on."

- James Callaghan

26

Visit the Allandale Mansion at Christmas

Allandale Mansion, Kingsport

"Christmas waves a magic wand over this world, and behold, everything is softer and more beautiful."

- Norman Vincent Peale

27

Stand in the Footsteps of History

National Civil Rights Museum at the Lorraine Motel, Memphis

"A man who won't die for something is not fit to live."

- Martin Luther King Jr.

28

Explore the Titanic

Titanic Museum, Pigeon Forge

"For a successful technology, reality must take precedence over public relations, for Nature cannot be fooled."

- Richard P. Feynman

29

Enjoy a Tall Tale

International Storytelling Center,
Jonesborough

"Don't tell fish stories where the people know you; but particularly, don't tell them where they know the fish."

- Mark Twain

30

Catch a Rising Star

The Bluebird Café, Nashville

"I believe that every person is born with talent."

- Maya Angelou

31

Tour a Winery

Anywhere, but Preferably on a Summer Afternoon

"Wine is constant proof that God loves us and loves to see us happy."

- Benjamin Franklin

32

See a Shark

Ripley's Aquarium of the Smokies, Gatlinburg

"By nature, I keep moving. My theory is, be the shark. You've just got to keep moving. You can't stop."

- Brad Pitt

33

Hear Al Green Preach

Full Gospel Tabernacle Church, Memphis

"The best and most beautiful things in the world cannon be seen or even touched - they must be felt with the heart."

- Helen Keller

34

Dance to the Tennessee Waltz

Anywhere

"The one thing that can solve most of our problems is dancing."

- James Brown

35

See the World's Oldest Nuclear Reactor

X-10 Nuclear Reactor, Oak Ridge

"It takes as much energy to wish as it does to plan."

- Eleanor Roosevelt

36

Visit Franklin on Foot

Downtown Franklin

"Not all those who wander are lost."

- J.R.R. Tolkien

37

See the General Lee

Cooter's Place, Gatlinburg

"Do your duty in all things. You cannot do more, you should never wish to do less."

- Robert E. Lee

38

Behold the Statue of Athena

The Parthenon, Centennial Park, Nashville

"Personal beauty is a greater recommendation than any letter of reference."

- Aristotle

39

Take a Workshop in Craftmaking

Appalachian Center for Craft, Cookeville

"Creativity is not the finding of a thing, but the making something out of it after it is found."

- James Russell Lowell

Author Michael Crisp and His Favorite Guitar.
Photo courtesy of Han Fan

40

Strum a Guitar

Gruhn Guitars, Nashville

"I've had three wives and three guitars. I still play the guitars."

- Andres Segovia

41

Buy a Freshwater Pearl

Tennessee River Freshwater Pearl Farm, Camden

"Men who have a pierced ear are better prepared for marriage - they've experienced pain and bought jewelry."

- Rita Rudner

42

See a College Football Game

Neyland Stadium, University of Tennessee, Knoxville

"Pressure is something you feel when you don't know what the hell you're doing."

- Peyton Manning

43

Visit a Planetarium

Bays Mountain Park & Planetarium, Kingsport

"Once you make a decision, the universe conspires to make it happen."

- Ralph Waldo Emerson

44

Play Miniature Golf

Anywhere in Gatlinburg or Pigeon Forge

"The only time my prayers are never answered are on the golf course."

- Billy Graham

45

Spend the Afternoon Shopping

Opry Mills Mall, Nashville

"When women are depressed, they eat or go shopping. Men invade another country. It's a whole different way of thinking."

- Elayne Boosler

46

Tour a Customs House

Customs House Museum & Cultural Center, Clarksville

"Wealth consists not in having great possessions, but in having few wants."

- Epictetus

47

Savor a MoonPie™

Anywhere, But Preferably with a RC Cola™

"Absolutely eat dessert first. The thing that you want to do the most, do that."

- Joss Whedon

48

See the Birthplace of Rock n Roll

Sun Studio, Memphis

"If I'm going to Hell, I'm going there playing the piano."

- Jerry Lee Lewis

49

Explore a Lost Sea

The Lost Sea, Sweetwater

"The water in a vessel is sparkling; the water in the sea is dark. The small truth has words which are clear; the great truth has great silence."

- Rabindranath Tagore

50

Create a Sculpture

Frist Center for the Visual Arts, Nashville

"The world is but a canvas to our imagination."

- Henry David Thoreau

51

Visit the Grave of Meriwether Lewis

Natchez Trace State Park, Wildersville

"As beautiful as simplicity is, it can become a tradition that stands in the way of exploration."

- Laura Nyro

52

See a Bear in the Woods

Anywhere, But Preferably in the Smoky Mountains

"The idea of wilderness needs no defense, it only needs defenders."

- Edward Abbey

53

Hike Along the Daniel Boone Wilderness Trail

Cumberland Gap National Historical Park

"I have never been lost, but I will admit to being confused for several weeks."

- Daniel Boone

54

Go Line Dancing

Wildhorse Saloon, Nashville

"The reward for conformity is that everyone likes you but yourself."

- Rita Mae Brown

55

Begin a Journey on the Appalachian Quilt Trail

Nathaniel Greene Museum, Greeneville

"As every thread of gold is valuable, so is every moment of time."

- John Mason

56

Spend the Day at Dollywood™

Pigeon Forge

"My weaknesses have always been food and men - in that order."

- Dolly Parton

57

Watch the Marching of the Ducks

The Peabody Hotel, Memphis

"Be like a duck. Calm on the surface, but always paddling like the dickens underneath."

- Michael Caine

58

Go Whitewater Rafting

Pigeon Forge River, Hartford

"What makes a river so restful to people is that it doesn't have any doubt - it is sure to get where it is going, and it doesn't want to go anywhere else."

- Hal Boyle

59

Experience Bonnaroo

Bonnaroo Music Festival, Manchester

"Love is a friendship set to music."

- Joseph Campbell

The Country Music Hall of Fame, Nashville
Photo courtesy of the Library of Congress

60

Visit the Country Music Hall of Fame

Country Music Hall of Fame, Nashville

"You got to have smelt a lot of mule manure before you can sing like a hillbilly."

- Hank WIlliams Sr.

61

Explore Market Square

Knoxville

"I learned to walk as a baby, and I haven't had a lesson since."

- Marilyn Monroe

62

Pig Out on Memphis-Style Barbecue

Memphis

"I am not a glutton - I am an explorer of food."

- Erma Bombeck

63

See the Night Lights

Cheekwood Botanical Garden &
Museum of Art, Nashville

"Middle age is when a guy keeps turning off lights for economical rather than romantic reasons."

- Lillian Gordy Carter

64

See an Eagle

Reelfoot Lake State Park, Tiptonville

"There is an eagle in me that wants to soar, and there is a hippopotamus in me that wants to wallow in the mud."

- Carl Sandburg

65

Sleep on a Train

Chattanooga Choo Choo, Historic Hotels of America, Chattanooga

"Neither a wise man nor a brave man lies down on the tracks of history to wait for the train of the future to run over him."

- Dwight D. Eisenhower

66

Discover the Mighty Mississippi

Mud Island River Park, Memphis

"Between flattery and admiration there often flows a river of contempt."

- Minna Antrim

67

Ride a Sky Lift

Gatlinburg

"There is the sky, which is all men's together."

- Euripedes

68

Picnic at Pickwick

Pickwick Landing State Park, Pickwick Dam

"Kissing a man with a beard is a lot like going to a picnic. You don't mind going through a little bush to get there!"

- Minnie Pearl

69

Visit the Jack Daniels™ Distillery

Lynchburg

"Always carry a flagon of whiskey in case of snakebite and furthermore always carry a small snake."

- W.C. Fields

70

Marvel at Ruby Falls

Lookout Mountain

"Over every mountain there is a path, although it may not be seen from the valley."

- Theodore Roethke

71

Sit in the "Scopes Monkey Trial" Courtroom

Dayton Courthouse, Dayton

"My theory of evolution is that Darwin was adopted."

- Steven Wright

72

Walk Across the Walnut Street Bridge

Chattanooga

"Mistakes are the usual bridge between inexperience and wisdom."

- Phyllis Theroux

73

See the Statue of Alex Haley

Knoxville

"Either you deal with what is the reality, or you can be sure that the reality is going to deal with you."

- Alex Haley

74

Sing "Rocky Top"

Or Dance to It If You Can't Carry a Tune in a Bucket

"My singing voice is somewhere between a drunken apology and a plumbing problem."

- Colin Firth

75

Tour a Plantation

Belle Meade Plantation, Nashville

"I like the dreams of the future better than the history of the past."

- Thomas Jefferson

76

See a Lady Vols™ Basketball Game

Thompson-Boling Arena, Knoxville

"Most people get excited about games, but I've got to be excited about practice, because that's my classroom."

- Pat Summitt

77

Tour the Home of a U.S. President

The Hermitage, Home of President Andrew Jackson, Nashville, The Andrew Johnson National Historic Site, Greeneville, and the James K. Polk House, Columbia

"There is no pleasure in having nothing to do; the fun is having lots to do and not doing it."

- Andrew Jackson

78

Fill Your Heart With Soul

Stax Museum of American Soul Music,
Memphis

"If a song's about something I've experienced or that could've happened to me, it's good. Because that's what soul is all about."

- Aretha Franklin

Space Needle, Gatlinburg
Photo courtesy of the Gatlinburg Space Needle

79

Ascend the Space Needle

Space Needle, Gatlinburg

"The scariest moment is always just before you start."

- Stephen King

80

See a Titans Game

LP Field, Nashville

"Football combines the two worst things about America: it is violence punctuated by committee meetings."

- George Will

81

Tread the Floor of the Memphis Cotton Exchange

The Cotton Museum at the Memphis Cotton Exchange, Memphis

"I wish they'd had electric guitars in cotton fields back in the good old days. A whole lot of things would've been straightened out."

- Jimi Hendrix

82

Cheer on the South (or North)

Dolly Parton's Dixie Stapede™, Pigeon Forge

"Standing in the middle of the road is very dangerous; you get knocked down by the traffic from both sides."

- Margaret Thatcher

83

Hear the Story of Casey Jones

Casey Jones Home & Railroad Museum, Jackson

"When the legends die, the dreams end; there is no more greatness."

- Tecumseh

84

Take a Riverboat Cruise at Night

Anywhere Along the Mississippi River

"The man who rows the boat seldom has time to rock it."

- Bill Copeland

85

Enjoy an Orchestra

Nashville Symphony, Schermerhorn Symphony Center, Nashville

"A symphony must be like the world. It must contain everything."

- Gustav Mahler

86

Get Married in a Wedding Chapel

Anywhere, but Preferably in Gatlinburg or Pigeon Forge

"Marriage is a wonderful institution, but who wants to live in an institution?"

- Groucho Marks

87

See a Grizzlies Game

FedExForum, Memphis

"When it gets down to it, basketball is basketball."

- Larry Bird

88

Sink Your Teeth into a King Leo™ Peppermint Stick

Anytime, but Preferably Around Christmas

"Sometimes I think that the one thing I love most about being an adult is the right to buy candy whenever and wherever I want."

- Ryan Gosling

89

Go Biking Down Roan Mountain

Johnson City

"May your trails be crooked, winding, lonesome, dangerous, leading to the most amazing view. May your mountains rise into and above the clouds."

- Edward Abbey

90

Walk the Halls of the Mabry-Hazen House

Mabry-Hazen House, Knoxville

"Be grateful for the home you have, knowing that at this moment, all you have is all you need."

- Sarah Ban Breathnach

91

See the Blue Hole Springs

Red Clay Tennessee State Historic Site, Cleveland

"A mouse never entrusts his life to only one hole."

- Plautus

92

Behold a Masterpiece

Brooks Museum of Art, Memphis

"Painting is just another way of keeping a diary."

- Pablo Picasso

93

Walk to the Top of Clingman's Dome

Great Smoky Mountains National Park, Pigeon Forge

"Never make your home in a place. Make a home for yourself inside your own head. You'll find what you need to furnish it - memory, friends you can trust, love of learning, and other such things. That way it will go with you wherever you journey."

- Tad Williams

94

Listen to a Country Music Concert

Ryman Auditorium, Nashville

"To me, there's two types of songs, good and bad. And I just like to stick with the good ones."

- Reba McEntire

95

Tour the George Dickel™ Distillery

Tullahoma

"Alcohol is necessary for a man so that he can have a good opinion of himself, undisturbed be the facts."

- Finley Peter Dunne

96

Ski the Slopes at Ober Gatlinburg

Gatlinburg

"Snow and adolescence are the only problems that disappear if you ignore them long enough."

- Earl Wilson

97

Visit a Fort

James White Fort, Knoxville

"Education is the cheap defense of nations."

- Edmund Burke

98

See a Show at the Orpheum

Orpheum Theatre, Memphis

"Music, in performance, is a type of sculpture. The air in the performance is sculpted into something."

- Frank Zappa

99

Learn About Lincoln

Abraham Lincoln Library & Museum,
Lincoln Memorial University, Harrogate

"In the end, it's not the years in your life that count. It's the life in your years."

- Abraham Lincoln

100

Share a Story With the Author of This Book

Anywhere, but Preferably on a Front Porch

"Laughter is not at all a bad beginning for a friendship, and it is far the best ending for one."

- Oscar Wilde

i did it

Check off your accomplishments with the writing utensil of your choice:

- ☐ 1. See a Show at the Grand Ole Opry
- ☐ 2. Behold the Beauty of a Tennessee Walker
- ☐ 3. Camp Out Under the Stars
- ☐ 4. Soak in the Hot Tub of a Rented Chalet
- ☐ 5. Watch a NASCAR™ Race
- ☐ 6. Sip Moonshine
- ☐ 7. Wander The District
- ☐ 8. Explore a King's Mansion
- ☐ 9. Be a Part of an Archeological Dig
- ☐ 10. See a Civil War Reenactment
- ☐ 11. Enjoy a Goo Goo Cluster™
- ☐ 12. See Seven States at the Same Time
- ☐ 13. Go Fly Fishing in Flat Fork Creek
- ☐ 14. Search for the Bell Witch
- ☐ 15. Take Your Family to the Pink Palace
- ☐ 16. Take a Walk Down Music Row
- ☐ 17. Visit the Home of Davy Crockett
- ☐ 18. See a Panda Bear
- ☐ 19. Devour a Bible Burger
- ☐ 20. Drive Under a Covered Bridge
- ☐ 21. Walk the Field at Shiloh
- ☐ 22. Explore Cades Cove
- ☐ 23. Stroll Down Beale Street

- ☐ 24. See the Sunsphere
- ☐ 25. Buy a Pair of Boots
- ☐ 26. Visit the Allandale Mansion at Christmas
- ☐ 27. Stand in the Footsteps of History
- ☐ 28. Explore the Titanic
- ☐ 29. Enjoy a Tall Tale
- ☐ 30. Catch a Rising Star
- ☐ 31. Tour a Winery
- ☐ 32. See a Shark
- ☐ 33. Hear Al Green Preach
- ☐ 34. Dance to the Tennessee Waltz
- ☐ 35. See the World's Oldest Nuclear Reactor
- ☐ 36. Visit Franklin on Foot
- ☐ 37. See the General Lee
- ☐ 38. Behold the Statue of Athena
- ☐ 39. Take a Workshop in Craftmaking
- ☐ 40. Strum a Guitar
- ☐ 41. Buy a Freshwater Pearl
- ☐ 42. See a College Football Game
- ☐ 43. Visit a Planetarium
- ☐ 44. Play Miniature Golf
- ☐ 45. Spend the Afternoon Shopping
- ☐ 46. Tour a Customs House
- ☐ 47. Savor a MoonPie™
- ☐ 48. See the Birthplace of Rock n Roll
- ☐ 49. Explore a Lost Sea
- ☐ 50. Create a Sculpture
- ☐ 51. Visit the Grave of Meriwether Lewis
- ☐ 52. See a Bear in the Woods
- ☐ 53. Hike Along the Daniel Boone Wilderness Trail

☐ 54. Go Line Dancing
☐ 55. Begin a Journey on the Appalachian Quilt Trail
☐ 56. Spend the Day at Dollywood™
☐ 57. Watch the Marching of the Ducks
☐ 58. Go Whitewater Rafting
☐ 59. Experience Bonnaroo
☐ 60. Visit the Country Music Hall of Fame
☐ 61. Explore Market Square
☐ 62. Pig Out on Memphis-Style Barbecue
☐ 63. See the Night Lights
☐ 64. See an Eagle
☐ 65. Sleep on a Train
☐ 66. Discover the Mighty Mississippi
☐ 67. Ride a Sky Lift
☐ 68. Picnic at Pickwick
☐ 69. Visit the Jack Daniels™ Distillery
☐ 70. Marvel at Ruby Falls
☐ 71. Sit in the "Scopes Monkey Trial" Courtroom
☐ 72. Walk Across the Walnut Street Bridge
☐ 73. See the Statue of Alex Haley
☐ 74. Sing "Rocky Top"
☐ 75. Tour a Plantation
☐ 76. See a Lady Vols™ Basketball Game
☐ 77. Tour the Home of a U.S. President
☐ 78. Fill Your Heart With Soul
☐ 79. Ascend the Space Needle
☐ 80. See a Titans Game
☐ 81. Tread the Floor of the Memphis Cotton Exchange

- ☐ 82. Cheer on the South (or North)
- ☐ 83. Hear the Story of Casey Jones
- ☐ 84. Take a Riverboat Cruise at Night
- ☐ 85. Enjoy an Orchestra
- ☐ 86. Get Married in a Wedding Chapel
- ☐ 87. See a Grizzlies Game
- ☐ 88. Sink Your Teeth into a King Leo™ Peppermint Stick
- ☐ 89. Go Biking Down Roan Mountain
- ☐ 90. Walk the Halls of the Mabry-Hazen House
- ☐ 91. See the Blue Hole Springs
- ☐ 92. Behold a Masterpiece
- ☐ 93. Walk to the Top of Clingman's Dome
- ☐ 94. Listen to a Country Music Concert
- ☐ 95. Tour the George Dickel™ Distillery
- ☐ 96. Ski the Slopes at Ober Gatlinburg
- ☐ 97. Visit a Fort
- ☐ 98. See a Show at the Orpheum
- ☐ 99. Learn About Lincoln
- ☐ 100. Share a Story With the Author of This Book

add to the list

- ☐ 101. ______
- ☐ 102. ______
- ☐ 103. ______
- ☐ 104. ______
- ☐ 105. ______
- ☐ 106. ______
- ☐ 107. ______
- ☐ 108. ______
- ☐ 109. ______
- ☐ 110. ______
- ☐ 111. ______
- ☐ 112. ______
- ☐ 113. ______
- ☐ 114. ______
- ☐ 115. ______
- ☐ 116. ______
- ☐ 117. ______
- ☐ 118. ______
- ☐ 119. ______
- ☐ 120. ______
- ☐ 121. ______
- ☐ 122. ______
- ☐ 123. ______
- ☐ 124. ______
- ☐ 125. ______

special thanks

Kevin Kifer
Scott Hall
Scott McBrayer
Andrew Moore
David Sloan
Kenny Rice
Han Fan
John McDaniel
Conner Crisp
Marge Crisp
Ryder McCraith
Pamela Holland
Karey Riddell
Dawn Brackman
Stacey Gillespie
Cindy McCain
Jim Byrge
David Rose
Old Crow Medicine Show
Bayless Family

The Tennessee Bucket List

written by

Michael Crisp

book jacket text and "what to expect" text written by Michael Crisp and David Sloan

Other Books by Michael Crisp

The Kentucky Bucket List

The Ohio Bucket List

Murder in the Mountains:
The Muriel Baldridge Story

The Making of The Very Worst Thing

Films Directed by Michael Crisp Include:

The Very Worst Thing

When Happy Met Froggie

Legendary: When Baseball
Came to the Bluegrass

A Cut Above: The Legend of Larry Roberts

Available at Local Bookstores
and Online at Amazon.com

"Though no one can go back and make a brand new start, anyone can start from now and make a brand new ending."

- Carl Bard